(4)

This book is to be r
the last date s

D1187880

1993

LEEDS CITY LIBRARIES DISCARDED

# About this book

Have you ever thought how the first railways were built?—moving mountains of earth to clear a level path for the line, laying the track, and building the stations along the route. Even a short railway would take years of back-breaking work. Yet between 1830 and 1860 the railway builders criss-crossed Britain with thousands of miles of new lines.

In this book you can see how the railways changed the lives of everyone living in Britain. You can learn, too, about the men who built the trains and bridges and laid the track. There were famous engineers like Isambard Brunel and George Stephenson, and also thousands of ordinary workers whose names are now forgotten. These were the railway navvies who worked day after day with pick and shovel, blasting and tunnelling and drinking and fighting their way across Britain. Find out for yourself what it was like to be one of the railway builders.

Some of the words printed in *italics* may be new to you. You can look them up in the word list on page 92.

AN EYEWITNESS BOOK

# The Railway Builders

ALISTAIR BARRIE

WAYLAND PUBLISHERS

# More Eyewitness Books

*Tutankhamun's Egypt*    Philippa Stewart
*The Story of Medicine*    Kathy & Mike Eldon
*Tom-tom to Television*    Kathy & Mike Eldon
*Toys in History*    Angela Schofield
*The Mayflower Pilgrims*    Brenda Colloms
*The Age of Drake*    Leonard Cowie
*Country Life in the Middle Ages*    Penelope Davies
*Growing up in the Middle Ages*    Penelope Davies
*Town Life in the Middle Ages*    Penelope Davies
*Markets and Fairs*    Jane Dorner
*Newgate to Tyburn*    Jane Dorner
*Kitchens and Cooking*    Kathy & Mike Eldon
*The Story of the Cinema*    Helen du Feu
*Road Transport*    Susan Goldblatt
*The Story of the Wheel*    Peter Hames
*Men in the Air*    Roger Hart
*The Voyages of Captain Cook*    Roger Hart
*Popular Entertainment*    Elizabeth Holt
*A Victorian Sunday*    Jill Hughes
*Livingstone in Africa*    Denis Judd
*Stagecoach and Highwayman*    Stephanie McKnight
*The Horseless Carriage*    Lord Montagu
*Shops and Shopping*    Ann Mountfield
*The Firefighters*    Ann Mountfield
*The Slave Trade*    Ann Mountfield
*Clothes in History*    Angela Schofield
*Shakespeare and his Theatre*    Philippa Stewart
*Sport Through the Ages*    Peter Wilson
*The Glorious Age of Charles II*    Helen Wodzicka
*The Printer and his Craft*    Helen Wodzicka
*Ships and Seafarers*    Helen Wodzicka

*Frontispiece:* The opening of the Stockton and Darlington Railway
            in 1825
First published 1973
Second impression 1977
SBN 85340 264 7
Copyright © 1973 by Wayland (Publishers) Ltd,
49 Lansdowne Place, Hove, East Sussex
Printed and bound in Great Britain by The Pitman Press, Bath

# Contents

# The First Railways

One hundred and fifty years ago, the first railways were opened. People came from far and near to gawp at the strange-looking boxes on wheels, pulled by a belching steam engine. The picture opposite shows a crowd of excited onlookers at the opening of the Canterbury and Whitstable Railway in 1830.

Many years before the first railways, businessmen had been trying to think of faster and cheaper ways to send their goods into the growing towns. Canals were the first great improvement in transport. The Duke of Bridgewater built a canal to send coal from his mines into Manchester. It was half the price to ship coal on the canal than to send it by road. After his success, many businessmen built canals.

But most passengers travelled by road, not by canal. The engineer Thomas Telford built many fine roads in Britain; John MacAdam invented a road surface that stopped highways from turning into mud tracks in rainy weather. But even the best stage-coaches only travelled as fast as the horses who pulled them—and horses only managed twelve miles per hour.

Then several inventors built a mechanical horse—the steam engine. A steam engine on rails travelled four times as fast as a horse, and pulled ten times the load. The first steam engines worked in the mines and on the docks. But then people realized that a railway could carry passengers as well. The first passenger railways were opened in the 1820s. They were built and owned by groups of businessmen, not by the government. They were the fastest and cheapest transport for one hundred years.

CANALS. Building a canal was a great feat of engineering. They cost a fortune to build, but they saved a lot of money for the owners who sent goods by *barge*. Before the railways came, businessmen built a network of canals all over England. This picture shows why canals were such a great success. On the road, four horses are struggling to pull a wagon filled with goods. But the horse alongside the canal is towing a loaded barge without any trouble.

WAGONS AND TRAMWAYS. The first railways began running in the 1820s. But the idea of running carts along on rails was not new. Horses had been towing wagons on rails for centuries before the steam engine was invented. The horses working at this coal mine in Northumberland are very lucky. They are only pulling empty wagons up the slope. They just trot behind the full ones as they roll down under their own weight. There were many small lines like this before railways were opened. Some of them took passengers and were called *tramways*.

CATCH-ME-WHO-CAN. Richard Trevithick, a Cornishman, was the real father of the steam engine. His first one ran on a tramway in Wales in 1804. It pulled five wagons loaded with 70 passengers and ten tons of iron. But the rails gave way under the weight. In 1809 he brought his engine to London. It was called *Catch me-who-can*, and Trevithick tried it out in the fields at Euston Square. As the picture opposite shows, curious Londoners came to Trevithick's "show," as if it were an oddity at a fair. But 30 years later, Euston Station was built on these same fields.

BLENKINSOP'S ENGINE. The inventor John Blenkinsop built the engine above in 1812. It ran on a special line $3\frac{1}{2}$ miles long, carrying coal between Middleton Colliery and the growing city of Leeds in Yorkshire. Inventors still thought engines needed a special toothed wheel to keep them on the rails and stop them crashing downhill. You can see the toothed wheel in the picture—it made the engine very slow. Blenkinsop's engine took an hour to get to Leeds. But it pulled 16 loaded wagons, many more than horses could pull.

*PUFFING BILLY*. This old photograph shows *Puffing Billy*. It pulled wagons of coal from Wylam Colliery to the ships on the River Tyne, fifteen miles away. William Hedley, who built *Puffing Billy*, didn't bother with the special toothed wheel Blenkinsop's engine used. The wheels were thick and the engine was heavy so *Puffing Billy* didn't jump off the rails. The locomotive was faster than Blenkinsop's engine, and it pulled coal wagons for fifty-two years before it was retired.

CURVES AND GRADIENTS.    Steam engines could pull greater loads than road wagons because they ran on rails. There was much less *friction* between the wheels and the rails. But engines had trouble on curves and *gradients*. In 1833, one engine pulled 67 tons on a level track, but couldn't move an inch on a slope of *1 in 12*. The train in this picture has special guide wheels to help it round corners. It is running on wooden rails, which were used on early tramways. But builders soon found that iron rails lasted longer and could bear heavier loads.

1. Before the collision—showing a train on its journey.

2. After the collision—showing two trains which have collided without harm to the passengers.

A SUGGESTION TO RAILWAY ENGINEERS.

CURIOUS INVENTIONS. On the first railways, there was always the danger that two engines would meet head on, or that one engine would crash into the back of another. There were few signalmen on the lines, and engines had poor brakes. Tunnels were especially dangerous. Trains went through at fixed times, although no one was sure if the tunnel was empty. These pictures show one inventor's idea for making collisions less dangerous for the passengers. Can you tell how the invention should work? But better brakes and signals were safer than inventions like this.

STEAM CARRIAGES. During the 1820s the railway engine had a rival—the steam carriage. Many people thought that steaming on ordinary roads was the last word in luxury travel. Thomas Telford, who built the great road from London to Holyhead, thought steam coaches were a much better idea than railway engines. But there was one great problem; in those days, roads were owned by private businessmen, and the road owners hated steam carriages. They raised their *tolls* to keep these "fiery monsters" off the roads.

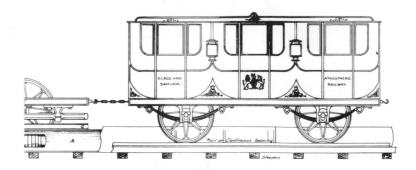

THE ATMOSPHERIC RAILWAY. Steam carriages didn't need rails. The "atmospheric railway" kept the rails but did away with steam. The inventors hoped to drive carriages along the rails by air pressure. There would be pipes running between the rails to keep up the pressure. In the early days of steam, engines were always breaking down and the atmospheric railway seemed a good idea. Isambard Brunel, who built the first railway from London to Bristol, liked this system better than steam engines. But it was impossible to keep the pressure up in bad weather, and no one could invent a way of crossing one line with another.

THE RAINHILL TRIALS. In 1829, the *directors* of the Liverpool and Manchester Railway wanted an engine to run long distances at high speeds for their new passenger railway. They decided to hold speed trials at Rainhill. The picture opposite shows the three engines that took part. The *Rocket*, at the top, was the most famous early steam engine. It reached a speed of 24 miles per hour on one run. The *Novelty* went faster, but halfway through the race it broke down. So the first prize of £500 was awarded to the *Rocket's* builder, George Stephenson. The *Rocket's* design became the model for all later steam engines.

# THE LOCOMOTIVE STEAM ENGINES,

WHICH COMPETED FOR THE PRIZE OF £500 OFFERED BY THE DIRECTORS OF THE LIVERPOOL AND MANCHESTER RAILWAY COMPANY

DRAWN TO A SCALE ¼ INCH TO A FOOT.

## THE "ROCKET" OF M.R ROB.T STEPHENSON OF NEWCASTLE,

WHICH DRAWING A LOAD EQUIVALENT TO THREE TIMES ITS WEIGHT TRAVELLED AT THE RATE OF 12½ MILES AN HOUR, AND WITH A CARRIAGE & PASSENGERS AT THE RATE OF 24 MILES.
COST PER MILE FOR FUEL ABOUT THREE HALFPENCE.

## THE "NOVELTY" OF MESS.RS BRAITHWAITE & ERRICSSON OF LONDON,

WHICH DRAWING A LOAD EQUIVALENT TO THREE TIMES ITS WEIGHT TRAVELLED AT THE RATE OF 20¼ MILES AN HOUR, AND WITH A CARRIAGE & PASSENGERS AT THE RATE OF 32 MILES.
COST PER MILE FOR FUEL ABOUT ONE HALFPENNY.

## THE "SANSPAREIL" OF M.R HACKWORTH OF DARLINGTON,

WHICH DRAWING A LOAD EQUIVALENT TO THREE TIMES ITS WEIGHT TRAVELLED AT THE RATE OF 12½ MILES AN HOUR, COST FOR FUEL PER MILE ABOUT TWO PENCE.

OPENING DAY. The Liverpool to Manchester Railway was the first modern one. Its owners offered to carry goods and passengers entirely by steam engine. Other railway companies used coaches and horses as well as engines. Opening day—15th September, 1830—was a national event. The Duke of Wellington, who was Prime Minister, rode in the first train which set out from Liverpool. A passenger named Mr Huskisson, who was a government minister, was run over by an engine and killed. Some people wanted to stop the opening celebrations, but the directors insisted that the train had to go on to Manchester. The people in the picture above are still waiting to cheer the first train in.

"RAIN, STEAM AND SPEED". The famous artist Joseph Turner painted the picture opposite of a steam engine crossing a viaduct about 1845. He called the painting "Rain, Steam and Speed". Turner wanted to show what an amazing invention the steam engine was. The engine is rushing across a viaduct in a fierce storm, travelling four times as fast as a stagecoach. It is man's answer to nature—faster even than a hare. The engine is just about to overtake a tiny hare on the viaduct. Can you see it?

# Liverpool and Manchester
# RAIL-WAY.

## TIME OF DEPARTURE

BOTH

# From Liverpool & Manchester.

| FIRST CLASS, FARE 5s. | SECOND CLASS, FARE 3s. 6d. |
|---|---|
| *Seven o'Clock Morning.* | *Eight o'Clock Morning.* |
| *Ten ,, Do.* | *Half-past Two Afternoon.* |
| *One ,, Afternoon.* | |
| *Half-past Four Do.* | |

\*\*\* For the convenience of Merchants and others, the First Class evening train of Carriages does not leave Manchester on *Tuesdays* and *Saturdays until Half-past Five o'Clock.*

The journey is usually accomplished by the First Class Carriages under two hours.

In addition to the above trains it is intended shortly to add three or four more departures daily.

The Company have commenced carrying GOODS of all kinds on the Rail-way.

*January,* 1831.

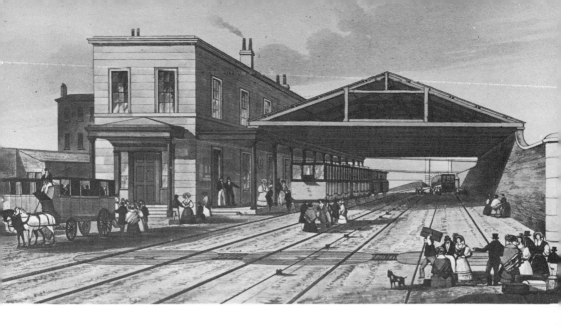

LIVERPOOL STATION. The picture above shows Liverpool Station—the first of the great passenger stations. Some passengers have just arrived by horse bus to join the first-class train to Manchester. Look at the railway carriages on the track. They look just like the horse buses on the left. The first railway carriages were stagecoaches on rails. Each carriage had its own name, just as the stagecoaches did. Instead of a bugler who always rode on a stagecoach, the new trains had a trumpeter who played as they pulled out of the station.

TIMETABLES. Opposite is the first timetable printed for the Liverpool and Manchester Railway. Despite the tragedy of the opening day, the railway was a great success. In the first three years, the trains carried 1,100 people a day between the two towns. All the road coaches travelling over the same route only carried 700 passengers a day between them. The Duke of Wellington was worried by the new-fangled invention. He said, "The railway is encouraging the lower orders to travel about."

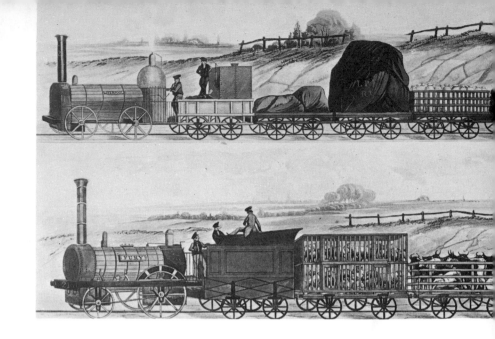

GOODS TRAFFIC. The directors of the Liverpool and Manchester Railway tried to win over as many passengers as they could for their trains. But they did a good trade in carrying goods as well. The two engines in the picture above are called the *Liverpool* and the *Fury*. They are pulling all kinds of goods. How many different things can you see? The owners are travelling in the wagons with their goods. Two farmers on the *Fury* are penned up with a herd of cattle. It must have been smelly and noisy.

SECOND-CLASS PASSENGERS. What was it like to ride on the first railway? Fanny Kemble, a young actress, said she closed her eyes and it felt like flying—"quite delightful!" But she was riding on the engine *footplate*, on a special journey. She wasn't squashed into an open carriage, like the travellers in the picture opposite. They are second-class passengers who paid 3s 6d (18½p) for the journey from Liverpool to Manchester. They had no protection from sudden downpours or howling winds. First-class passengers paid 5s (25p) and sat in closed carriages.

STEAMED OUT. "Pray remember the coachmen," says the driver in this cartoon. He speaks for everyone who lost their passengers and jobs to the railways. Grooms, stable boys, postboys and innkeepers were thrown out of work, as well as drivers. The blow was much worse because it happened so suddenly. Stagecoaches and roads had been improving all the time, but no coach could travel as fast as a train or carry as many passengers. Coaches disappeared from the roads in about 15 years. Even the mail coaches, the best of all, had stopped running by the 1840s.

COACH AND STEAM. The coachmen put up a fight on some routes against the railway. On the busy route to Ireland, there was room for both until about 1850. The stagecoach in this picture is running on the best road in Britain. Thomas Telford had built it only 20 years earlier. Coaches could keep up an average speed of 12 miles per hour on this road. But Robert Stephenson built a railway which travelled much faster. You can see a train running alongside the sea, 250 feet below the road.

# The Engineers

By 1851, the year of the Great Exhibition, most large towns in Victorian England boasted a rail link with London. Huge sums of money were sunk into these railways. First, the company directors had to get their schemes approved by Parliament. There were often protests from coaching companies, landowners and private road owners. Land was expensive, too. The London and Birmingham railway company paid £6,000 per mile. When local people objected to the railways, there were costly delays: one vicar allowed the railway over his land in return for a promise of four bridges. He really didn't want the bridges. He later received £20,000 from the company in return for not building them!

Engineers were at the centre of all this activity. They had complete charge of the building operation. The engineer made the *survey* and chose the best route. He also picked the *contractors* who agreed to build part of the line for a fixed price. The engineer spent his day supervising the works along the line. He was like a general, battling to take the railway through. Sometimes he even fought real battles. One contractor on the Great Western Railway was sacked from his job, but he refused to budge from the tunnel he was building. Isambard Brunel, the engineer, led his *navvies* to take over the tunnel by force. After some fighting, the contractor agreed to go.

The railway engineers made mistakes, but their decisions were usually right. Today's electric loco-motives still run along the same routes and over bridges they charted and built.

GEORGE STEPHENSON.   George Stephenson was the first of the great engineer builders. He began his working life as a pit boy at Killingworth Colliery near Newcastle. He learned all about pit railways and he became very skilled at building steam engines. Then he convinced the directors of the Stockton and Darlington Railway Company that he was the man to build and run their railway. With his son Robert helping him, he went on to build the Liverpool and Manchester Railway. In this picture, he is teaching the navvies about railway building.

OLIVE MOUNT. At Olive Mount, George Stephenson and his navvy builders had to take the Liverpool and Manchester Railway through solid rock. They blasted their way through with gunpowder. This painting shows one of the first trains chugging through the steep and narrow walls of rock. You can see the navvies working with pick and shovel on the jagged rocks above the track, to make the cutting.

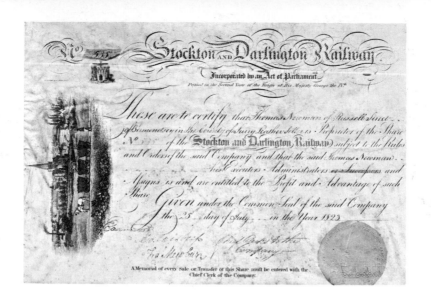

RAILWAY MANIA. "Railway mania" was a mad rush to build railways. During the 1830s and 40s, businessmen and *investors* fought to buy railway *shares* because they thought that a railway built anywhere in the world was sure to make a profit. The magazine *Punch* printed a report about an imaginary railway that would run from Land's End to John O' Groats. The picture opposite is an imaginary scene: it shows the railway planners pushing and shoving outside the Board of Trade. They all want to show their schemes to the Board and get its approval.

SHAREHOLDERS. A railway like the Great Western from London to Bristol cost £6½ million to build. The directors could only get these vast sums by asking the public to loan them money. The public bought shares, and they received certificates like the one in the picture above. They ran the risk of losing money if a company collapsed, but all the railways made profits in the 1840s. Each year, the companies paid shareholders a dividend, or a part of the profits. Thousands of people invested in the railways during the years of railway mania.

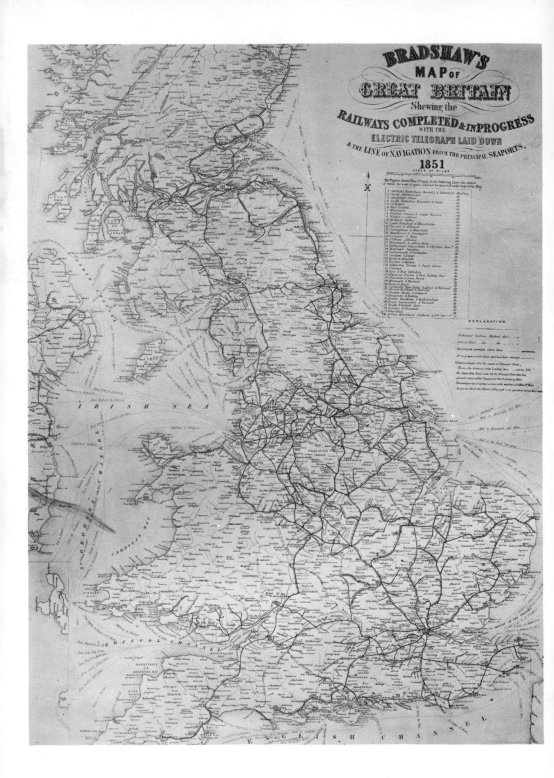

CELEBRATION DINNERS. Every railway company celebrated the opening of its railway with a grand dinner. This dinner was held after the Carlisle and Lancaster Railway was opened. Few of the railway builders would be guests at a dinner like this. The directors invited the shareholders who had loaned them large sums. The navvies were never invited, though some companies stood them bread, cheese and beer at a local pub. These guests have eaten well, and the directors are just about to make their speeches describing the new railway.

NEW RAILWAYS. George Bradshaw was famous for his railway maps and timetables. He made the map on the left of the railways in Britain in 1851. As you can see, many lines were built by this time. A passenger could travel from London to Plymouth in the West on the line built by Isambard Brunel. Brunel had plans to take the railway into Cornwall. A passenger could travel to Holyhead on Robert Stephenson's line, and then catch the boat to Ireland. There were two routes into Scotland. Besides these major lines there was a maze of smaller ones that criss-crossed the country.

EUSTON ARCH. Some railway companies did more than hold a mere dinner to celebrate their railways. This picture shows the great arch at Euston in London. It towered above Euston Station, the *terminus* of the London and Birmingham Railway. The directors hired a famous architect to design it and spent £35,000 building it. Euston Arch said more about their pride in the new railway than a hundred after-dinner speeches. It was finally pulled down in 1960 when British Rail built a new station at Euston.

EUSTON STATION. This picture shows Euston Station in 1837, the year Queen Victoria came to the throne. The London and Birmingham Railway had first and second-class passengers on the same train, something new in those days. But the second-class carriages were still open to the weather. As you can see, there isn't an engine in sight. For the first $1\frac{1}{2}$ miles out of Euston Station, the gradient was too steep for steam engines. So the carriages were pulled up the slope by cables and joined the engine at the top.

RAILWAYS FOR THE RICH.   This engine steaming along the London and Birmingham Railway about 1838 is pulling all sorts of different carriages. There is even a separate wagon to carry a gentleman's private coach! The railway companies were trying to attract rich passengers. At this time, many people in the upper classes agreed with the Duke of Wellington that rail travel was "for the lower orders." But the Duke changed his mind when he was allowed to take his own coach on the train. He never sat in a public carriage again. He had his own coach loaded onto the train and rode in it throughout the journey.

CONTRACTING.   The bridge in the picture opposite was one of many built under contract on Robert Stephenson's London and Birmingham Railway. On such a long railway the engineer could not supervise all the building himself. So he offered different sections of the line to other men known as contractors. The contractors agreed to build a tunnel, bridge or several miles of track at a fixed price. Then they hired workmen and got on with the job. Sometimes the contractor made a good profit. But he could also lose money. Thomas Brassey, the most famous contractor, had to rebuild a bridge which had collapsed. He paid the whole cost of rebuilding from his own pocket.

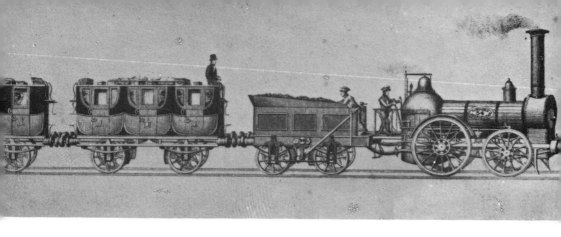

BRITANNIA BRIDGE. This picture shows the great bridge on the London, Chester and Holyhead Railway. Robert Stephenson built it to span the Menai Straits between the north Welsh coast and the Island of Anglesey. The bridge is a long tube held up by four towers. The biggest tower stands on the Britannia rock which gave the bridge its name. First the navvies built the towers, and then floated the tubes downstream in sections. They planned to raise the tubes on the towers, but they ran into trouble. The tide threatened to sweep the tubes out to sea. Local people watching from the banks rushed to help hold the tubes back.

THE LAST RIVET. Robert Stephenson himself drove in the last of the two million rivets which hold the Britannia Bridge together. This rivet was painted white for the occasion, and it is still kept white today. Robert Stephenson was certainly glad to finish the job. He once wrote that he couldn't sleep for thinking about the tubes, and wondering whether the bridge would hold up. He need not have worried. Britannia Bridge carries heavy traffic today, even after a fire which closed it down for several months in 1970.

ROUND DOWN CLIFF. The railway engineers could blast, tunnel and dig their way through just about everything. Round Down Cliff used to stand in the way of this railway from Folkstone to Dover. It was 375 feet high. Tunnelling was too expensive and digging would have taken too long. The engineer, William Cubitt, decided to blast it away. The navvies bored holes and packed 19,000 pounds of gunpowder into the cliff. The directors invited guests to watch the explosion. The cliff took only two minutes to disappear—it was blown to bits and just dissolved into the sea.

ISAMBARD KINGDOM BRUNEL. Like Robert Stephenson, Brunel had a famous engineer for a father. Young Isambard's first engineering job was helping his father, Mark Brunel, to build a footway under the River Thames. He was still a young man when the directors of the Great Western Railway asked him to fill the post of engineer. Brunel, whom you can see on the right, did not just build railways. He also built several great steamships and famous road bridges. His best-known road bridge is the Clifton Suspension Bridge which spans the Avon Gorge at Bristol.

BRUNEL

BRUNEL'S "BILLIARD TABLE." Brunel set out
to prove himself as an engineer on the Great Western
Railway. He did not think much of the power of the
steam engine. So he decided not to give his route
any gradient which an engine could not climb easily.
This meant longer tunnels and deeper *cuttings* than
other engineers had built. When the line was finished,
some people called it "Brunel's billiard table"
because it was so flat. It was almost dead level for
the first 85 miles out of London. Brunel's men are
making one of the deep cuttings in this picture.

MAIDENHEAD BRIDGE. Taking the Great Western Railway across the Thames at Maidenhead was a problem. The Thames officials insisted that Brunel had to build a bridge that wouldn't get in the way of river traffic. So Brunel built the bridge you can see here. It has very wide, flat arches to allow many boats to pass through at the same time. Some people in Maidenhead hoped the bridge would collapse. They were the owners of the road bridge you can see at the back. They were afraid that all the travellers and goods would go by rail and their bridge would be empty.

BOX TUNNEL.   Brunel left the hardest section of
the London to Bristol line till last. Part of it ran
through Box Hill, between Chippenham and Bath.
Brunel realized he would have to build a two-mile
tunnel through the hill. One and a half miles of Box
Hill was soft rock and clay. The contractor who agreed
to build this part of the tunnel finished on time, even
though he used more than thirty million bricks to
line the roof and sides. The last half-mile was solid
Bath stone. The navvies used a ton of gunpowder

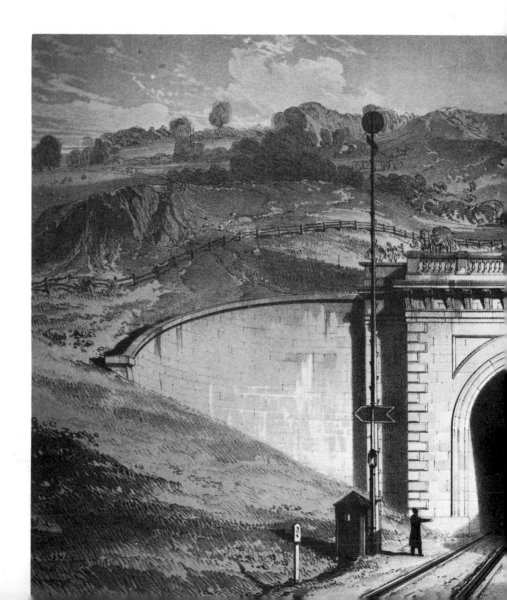

and a ton of candles every day for two and a half years, blasting their way through. Brunel was inside the tunnel when the two gangs working towards each other finally met. He was so pleased that he gave his ring to the foreman in charge. But the troubles weren't over. A famous *geologist*, Dr. Buckland, said that the tunnel would collapse from the vibrations of the engines. Luckily, he was wrong. In June, 1841, the first train left Paddington Station and passed through Box Tunnel to arrive in Bristol in four hours.

ROYAL ALBERT BRIDGE. Brunel's most famous railway bridge is the Royal Albert. It crosses the River Tamar which separates Cornwall from the rest of England. The navy wanted the bridge one hundred feet high to keep clear of ships. Brunel designed the bridge on two separate tubes, each holding half the track. He built a brick pier in the centre of the channel to join the two halves. His men put the tubes together on the river bank, and then floated them into position on rafts. In the old photograph opposite, the second tube still has to be raised. It went up slowly, inch by inch, as the men built up a pier at this end.

BRUNEL'S LAST LOOK. This is a painting of the Royal Albert Bridge after it was finished. Brunel never saw his bridge open for traffic. Years of travel, work and worry had ruined his health. He was too ill to see to the raising of the second tube, and he didn't go to the opening ceremony. But he did see the finished bridge once. Lying on a special flat wagon, an engine slowly drew him beneath the iron girders for a last look. He died four months later.

# The Railway Navvies

The men who dug the tunnels and laid the track for the railways were the navvies. They got their name from the old navigators who built canals fifty years before. The famous contractor Thomas Brassey had thousands of navvies working for him. He said it took a year to make a skilled navvy out of an ordinary working man.

A navvy took a twelve hour shift in his stride, even if he was working in a damp dark tunnel. In a full day's work, he could shovel out twenty tons of earth and fill seven railway wagons. Navvies ate two pounds of best beef and drank a gallon of beer a day to keep them going at this rate.

But navvying was more than just a job. The men who worked at railway building had given up a settled way of life. They lived alongside the lines they built. When they finished one railway they tramped off to build another. They even went abroad—British navvies built thousands of miles of railways all over the world, including India and South America.

Navvies had many customs. They gave each other strange nicknames. They had their own kind of wedding. Instead of a service in church, the bride and groom jumped over a broomstick. After a *pay*, many navvies spent days drinking, and they all got into trouble for *poaching*. Navvies fought among themselves and their battles terrified people in the quiet villages. In Penrith, Cumberland, in 1846, English and Irish navvies got into fights and terrorized the villagers for a week.

BLASTING ROCKS. The navvies often had to take the railway through solid rock. It was impossible for them to dig their way through with pick and shovel: they had to blast the rocks aside. The navvies drilled holes in the rock and packed them with gunpowder. They sealed off the holes with clay to make a bigger explosion. One navvy sounded a bugle to warn the others, and then lit the fuse. This picture shows navvies blasting rock at Linslade on the London and Birmingham line. Can you imagine the noise of bugles and explosions?

MAKING A CUTTING. The navvies had to lay the tracks as level as possible because engines lost all their power pulling trains up gradients. Sometimes, navvies had to build tunnels or embankments. At other times they made a cutting by digging a long and deep path through the hillside for the tracks. This picture shows navvies making a cutting at Tring in Hertfordshire. It is already 40 feet deep and runs for $2\frac{1}{2}$ miles. You can see the navvies running up the sides with wheelbarrows full of earth. They must be dizzy from the slope.

MAKING THE RUN. Only the strongest navvies could "make the run." It was often the only way to get the earth out of a cutting as the navvies dug deeper and deeper. Look at the picture: the navvy "making the run" tied ropes round himself and his wheelbarrow full of earth. Then the ropes were passed through the pulleys at the top of the slope and tied to a horse. A man next to the pulley gave a signal for the horses to start pulling. Man and barrow raced up the wooden slope to tip the load into a wagon on top.

EMBANKMENTS. Navvies were sometimes called "bankers" because part of their job was making embankments. An embankment was a cutting in reverse. Instead of cutting down into the hillside, the navvies had to build up a long mound of earth to keep the railway track level. The navvies often used earth which they had dug out of a cutting further down the line. The engine steaming along the embankment in the picture is carrying more earth. The navvies will tip it down the slope to make the embankment longer.

STARTING A TUNNEL. The navvies usually began by digging several *shafts* along the route the tunnel was to follow. They used a machine like the one in the picture, called a horse gin. It was a huge wooden drill attached to a great wheel. The two horses plodded round and round to make the power which turned the wheel. This machine could dig a shaft 10 feet wide and 600 feet deep. Next, the navvies lowered themselves into the darkness in buckets. They made the shaft bigger by digging and blasting.

BLASTING UNDERGROUND. These navvies are working at the bottom of a tunnel shaft. The two men on the left are boring a hole in the rock to hold the gunpowder. The men on the right are *stemmers*. They rammed the powder into the hole. It was a more dangerous job than it sounds. In some tunnels, the stemmers used iron rods to pack in the powder. The rods sometimes struck against the rocks and made sparks. The gunpowder exploded—and many navvies were killed or *maimed*.

DANGEROUS WORK. As the shafts got larger, the navvies had more room to work, and more light. But they were still in danger from sudden falls of earth or explosions. So many navvies were killed at the Woodhead Tunnel that the Government held an *enquiry*. The investigators reported that men were killed falling out of buckets as they were lowered down the shafts. This picture shows the Kilsby Tunnel on the London and Birmingham railway. Three navvies here played follow the leader, jumping across an open shaft. None of them made it. They all fell through, one after another.

FINISHING OFF. The navvies in this picture are
putting the finishing touches on the Kilsby Tunnel.
They look tiny inside the huge shaft. You can just
pick them out, working on the brickwork half-way up.
Because the shaft was open at the top, a constant
gale blew through the tunnel. It couldn't have been
very pleasant for the navvies, but it was better than
digging a tunnel in the pitch dark.

TUNNEL APPROACHES.   There was more to tunnel
building than digging and blasting at the bottom of
shafts. These navvies are banking up the earth and
laying the track at the approaches to a tunnel.
Skilled bricklayers and stonemasons have built the
grand tunnel entrance: Navvies are still working
inside the tunnel, but they don't have to send the
earth up the shafts in buckets. They can now load
it into wagons which horses pull along the tracks.

UNDER THE RIVERS   The navvies had to put up with the cold, dark and wet when they built tunnels under water. These men are working on the Severn Tunnel, which took the railway into Wales. Water was always trickling into the shafts, and the men had to keep the pumps going all the time. They worked in constant fear of a flood. Even a good day's work would only add a few feet to the tunnel. It took 14 years to build the Severn Tunnel, $4\frac{1}{2}$ miles long. There was even a flood after the tunnel opened, when a stream of water broke through a brick wall two feet thick.

ST. PANCRAS CHURCHYARD. This picture shows navvies working at St. Pancras Churchyard in London—they had to take the railway right through the graves. The Bishop of London insisted that the navvies had to be respectful to the dead. Screens were put up so passers-by could not see what they were doing. Behind the screens, the navvies worked day and night at the grim task of digging up and reburying the bodies in new coffins. The relatives of a Frenchman buried here asked for his body to be sent back to France. But the navvies found three different corpses in his grave! The navvy foreman was sure that foreigners' bones were blacker than English ones. So he sent the darkest ones to France.

NAVVY'S CLOTHES. Sometimes navvies found themselves between railway jobs. Then they built docks, reservoirs or even roads. The men in this photograph worked on the Crystal Palace, the vast building of glass and iron where the Great Exhibition was held. But they were still railway navvies. They thought they were better than ordinary workers, and they dressed to show it. Look at the man on the left. Navvies paid 15s (75p) for a peaked cap like his, a lot of money in those days. Waistcoats, well-made shirts, trousers tied at the knee and strong, hob-nailed boots were all part of the navvy's uniform.

ON THE MOORS. Navvies tramped on because they didn't like to work in lonely, deserted spots, like Chat Moss in the picture above. If they were building a tunnel, they might have to spend years out on the moors and make their own shelters. The navvies who worked at Woodhead near Sheffield didn't even have tents when they started. They had to sleep out in the open for a month. Food was scarce and expensive because the navvies could only buy it in the towns. Woodhead was an unhealthy place. The navvies paid for a doctor, but *cholera* swept through the camp. Twenty-eight navvies died and the survivors ran away in terror.

TRAMPING. Moving on was part of a navvy's life. A navvy would up and leave the railway works if he had a row with his foreman, or if he heard of better pay somewhere else. He might get drunk after a *pay*, drift away from the line and forget to go back. A navvy who arrived at a *contract* was welcomed by the railway builders there. They were eager to hear the tramping navvy's news about other works. If the new navvy couldn't find a job, his fellow workers collected money for him.

IN THE CITIES. The navvies had an easier life when they built railways in cities or towns. They could find lodgings near the works and they could buy food in local shops. They were not at the mercy of sharp traders who sold poor quality food at high prices to navvies on the moors. Navvies in town could choose their own pubs. They did not have to drink the contractor's watered-down beer. But railway building was still grim and hard work, as you can see from this picture of navvies laying track near King's Cross in London.

NEIGHBOURHOODS IN DANGER. Charles Dickens, the famous novelist, went to see the new railway works at Camden Town in London. The picture shows the navvies building a *retaining wall* at Camden. Dickens thought the works looked like an earthquake. He described all the houses knocked down, the streets broken through, the deep pits, and the enormous heaps of earth lying about. "There are thousands of tunnels, everything looks chaotic," he said. How do you think the families living in the nearby houses felt about the new railway?

NAVVIES AT WAR. Navvies became national heroes after they built a railway at Balaclava in the Crimea. You can see them working on the line in the picture above. This was in 1855, when Britain, France and Turkey were at war with Russia. The British army was bogged down in front of Sevastapol, laying siege to the city. The navvies' railway brought vital supplies of food and medicine to the soldiers and kept them alive during the bitter Crimean winter.

WORKING AT BALACLAVA. The navvies at work in the picture opposite broke all records building the line at Balaclava. Ten days after arriving in the Crimea, they had finished the huts next to the line and had laid the first few miles of track. People at home compared the navvies' success with the failure of the British soldiers there. About 350 navvies had shipped out from Liverpool, well-equipped and keen to work. They were steady men who sent £1 of their wages to their families every week.

# Railways in Britain

The first railways were built in Britain, and this was no accident. At that time, Britain was the only country which could find the men, money and materials to build them. Britain had reserves of money from colonial trade, and stocks of coal and iron ore, She also had thousands of men who had lost their jobs farming the land. They became some of the 200,000 railway navvies.

Building the railways helped other industries all over the country. The brick-makers of Chippenham were busy for $2\frac{1}{2}$ years supplying the bricks for Box Tunnel—all 30 million of them! The iron and steel industries provided metal for tracks and bridges. The coal industry grew as more coal was needed to power the steam engines.

As the railways grew into a national transport system, every industry sent their goods cheaply by rail. Railways brought new jobs and buildings to the towns and villages, and turned them into bustling cities. They also brought travel within the reach of ordinary people who could never have afforded the journey by coach or horse. During the 19th century railways became safer and more comfortable, and more and more people travelled on them. The picture opposite shows Paddington Station in 1851. Look at all the different kinds of people about to board the train. The railway was barely twenty years old but it was already a part of life in Britain.

NEW JOBS. There were many new jobs in England because of the railways, such as building engines. This is a view of the engine factory which Robert Stephenson set up in Newcastle in the 1820s. The workmen here made all the engines which ran on the Stockton and Darlington and Liverpool and Manchester Railways in the early years. More and more engines were needed as new railways were opened. Thousands of people worked at building engines in factories at Manchester, Wolverton, Swindon, Derby and Crewe.

BIGGER ENGINES. These men are working at a factory in Manchester in 1852. They are building an engine for the London and Northwestern Railway. This engine is much heavier than the *Rocket* which George Stephenson built for the Rainhill Trials. The *Rocket* had been the first engine fast enough for passenger trains, but engine-makers soon made better ones. Then the railway builders began to lay steel rails, which could take much bigger and heavier engines. The engines which raced to Scotland in 1881 averaged more than 60 miles an hour on the journey.

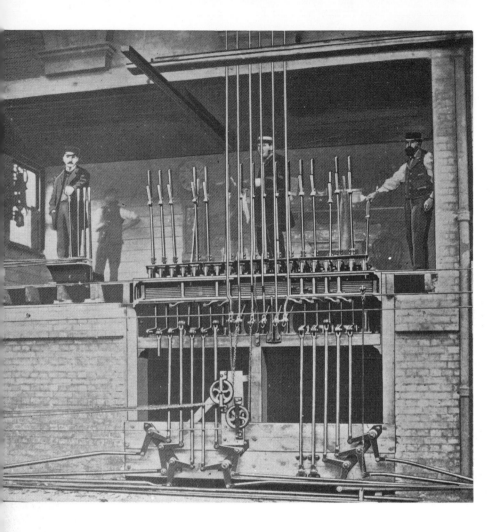

SIGNALS.   Signalling was another new job. The first railways did not use many signals. Instead, a few men stood on the track to make signs to the engine-drivers to tell them if the way was clear. Sometimes they rang a bell to warn people that a train was approaching. As soon as lines began to cross over one another, this simple arrangement became danger-ous. The signals at this busy *junction* are greatly improved. The men use levers and rods to control signals which tell the drivers to stop, or to go on carefully.

PLATE-LAYERS. These men are dressed rather like navvies but their job is quite different. They are plate-layers. The railway companies paid them to keep the track in good order so that the trains would run smoothly and safely. On this morning, though, they are taking up the last of the old *broad gauge* track near the Royal Albert Bridge at Saltash. Broad gauge was the track width that Brunel liked best, but it finally disappeared from British railways. Standard gauge track took its place.

CARRYING THE MAIL. The London and Manchester was the first railway to carry letters and parcels regularly. It began this service in 1830. At first, it was just an experiment, but in 1839 the government passed an Act entrusting railways with the Royal Mail. After 1839, people could send a letter anywhere in Britain for exactly one penny. It would never have been possible to deliver mail at such a low price without the railways to carry letters all over the country. This picture shows the first air pressure railway for the mail. It carried letters from a sorting office straight to Euston Station.

RUNNING THE RAILWAYS. Thousands of people found jobs on the new railways. Think of all the clerks selling tickets at stations all over Britain. This old photograph was taken in 1876. It shows some of the men who worked at Earl's Court in London on the old Circle Line. You can see stationmen, porters, drivers and signalmen. The gentlemen in the top hat is an engine inspector. He was in charge of all the engines running on the line.

NEW TOWNS. When Brunel built the railway from London to Bristol, Swindon was a small market town on the route. But Brunel chose Swindon as the mid-point of the line—the best place to change engines and carry out repairs. He built workshops there and streets of houses for the workers and their families. There were many villages like Swindon which grew into large towns with the coming of the railways. Crewe, Barrow, Wolverton and Derby were some of the others.

TOWN AND COUNTRY. The railways kept the countryfolk in touch with the rest of England by carrying the mail. People in small villages could write to friends living far away. Railways also brought the countryfolk into towns and cities. Even tiny villages had a station, like Berkhampstead in the picture. It was on the railway which Robert Stephenson built from London to Birmingham. The family leaving the station might have visited London. Before the railway came, they probably would never have left their village.

THE GREAT EXHIBITION. 1851 was the year
when the country people came up to London. Six
million of them flocked in mostly by rail, to see the
Great Exhibition at the Crystal Palace. Prince Albert,
Queen Victoria's husband, thought up the idea of a
great fair to show products from all over the world.
He did much to organize the Exhibition, but it was
the railways who made the building and brought

tho people. Crystal Palace was like a giant railway station, made of iron and glass. It was three-quarters of a mile long! The architect, Joseph Paxton, jotted down the design in a spare moment at a railway directors' meeting in Manchester. Railway navvies put it up in Hyde Park, and railway companies ran excursion trains at cheap fares so people from all over the country could see the Exhibition.

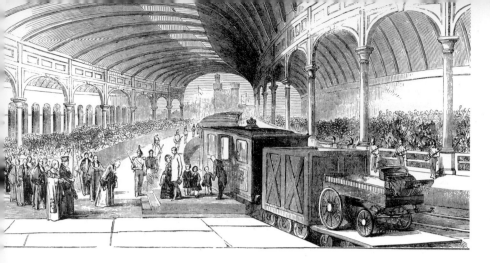

ROYAL TRAVELLERS. Queen Victoria first travelled by rail in 1842. She made the journey from Windsor Castle to Paddington Station in London on the new Great Western Railway. Her journey was a great triumph for the railways. If the Queen used trains, who could say they were only for the lower classes? But the Queen didn't travel quite like other passengers. She rode in a special train, and she always had a grand reception at the end of her journey. The picture above shows the Queen arriving in Newcastle. In 1869, one company built a magnificent set of railway carriages for the Queen. You can still see them at the British Transport Museum in London.

DIFFERENT CLASSES. The railways had three-class trains until 1867 when the Midland Railway did away with the third-class. Look at the pictures opposite—the railway directors thought that the three classes matched the different kinds of passengers. The rich rode in comfortable and uncrowded first-class carriages. More passengers were packed into second-class, but it was much cheaper. The third-class passengers look pretty rowdy. Parliament passed an Act which said that all travellers had to be protected from the weather, but this railway company still has open carriages for these unlucky passengers in the picture opposite.

RIVALRY. The railways in Britain were not owned by the government in the 19th century. They were private companies and they had to make a profit. They fought bitterly for a bigger share of the passengers and the goods. Sometimes the passengers benefited from the rivalry—they paid cheaper fares as the railways cut their prices to attract more travellers. But passengers usually found the rivalry tiresome. Two large groups of railway companies had different widths of track. It was impossible for the trains of one group to run on the rails of the other. The picture shows porters transferring goods and parcels from one train to another train which ran on different sized track.

LANDSLIPS. More and more people began to travel by rail for pleasure. Whole families took excursion trains into the country or to the seaside. Sometimes, these outings ran into trouble. In this picture, an excursion train running on the South Devon Railway has come to a sudden stop—a landslip is blocking the line. Huge rocks are piled up on the track. The passengers have clambered out of the carriages and are settling down for a long wait. Can you see the boy making his tea?

DISASTERS. There were many accidents on the early railways. The drawing above shows the crash at Abergele, a small village on the coast of north Wales. An engine-driver left some wagons full of petrol right in the path of a fast train from London. The train crashed into the wagons and went up in flames. Within seconds, fire swept through the first four wooden carriages. At this time, passengers were usually locked in the train compartments between stations. Thirty-two people died in this crash because they couldn't get out of the train.

CHANGING CITIES. Look at the difference between the two cities shown opposite. The top picture is Newcastle in 1750. At the bottom is Stockport, one hundred years later. The changes brought by the railways were plain to see in the cities. The waterfront in Newcastle looks quiet and peaceful. It is still lined with the old pointed-roof houses of the medieval traders. There is little dirt or grime. Stockport is completely over-shadowed by the great railway arches. The railway brought new industry to the city, and the factory chimneys are belching out thick smoke.

OVERGROUND AND UNDERGROUND. The London and Greenwich was one of the earliest railways. The first section from Deptford to London Bridge opened in 1836. It was the first "city railway." The builders put it up on a platform of brick arches to carry it over the house-tops. This railway took workers to the centre of London in the morning and brought them home to the outskirts in the evening. In later years, builders put these railways under the streets. The overground and underground railways changed the lives of city-dwellers. Now they could live in one part of a city and work in another section.

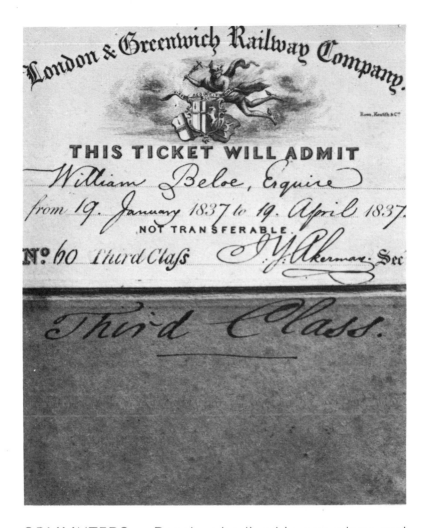

London & Greenwich Railway Company.

THIS TICKET WILL ADMIT

*William Beloe, Esquire*

*from 19. January 1837 to 19. April 1837.*

NOT TRANSFERABLE.

Nº 60 *Third Class*

*Third Class.*

COMMUTERS.   People who lived in one place and worked in another had to make regular journeys every day. The London and Greenwich was the first company to offer special fares to regular passengers. They were called commuters. Commuting means bargaining for a cheaper fare in return for making daily journeys. The man who bought this season ticket was one of the first commuters. Nowadays, a commuter is anyone who makes the same journey to work each day. In the 19th century, commuters always travelled by rail.

THE RAILWAY BOOKSELLER.  William Smith was a London newsagent. In 1851, he promised to pay the London and Northwestern Railway £1,700 a year for the right to sell all the newspapers and books at the company's stations. In 1862, he managed to get the same rights on the other main railway lines. Smith's business grew as more people learned to read and more of them travelled by rail. This old photograph shows newsboys outside a W. H. Smith book-shop in 1906.

ADVERTISING MANIA. A railway station was a marvellous place to advertise. Where else could posters reach so many people? Workmen, gentlemen and even royalty were all bound to travel by rail sometime or other. The artist who drew this picture thought the advertisers had got out of hand. In his imaginary station, the walls have been plastered with advertisements from floor to ceiling.

EXCURSIONS. The outing by rail was Thomas Cook's idea. He thought it up while he was walking to a meeting 15 miles from his home. Why not hire a train and charge special rates for anyone who wanted to go? Next time he did just that and the trip was a great success. Thomas Cook's idea caught on, and the railway companies began to copy him. This picture shows cityfolk on an excursion to the seaside. Excursions gave working people a chance to escape from the grime of the new industrial towns. Because of the railways, they were able to travel for pleasure, just as we do today.

# Table of Dates

# New Words

| | |
|---|---|
| *A contract* | Name for a railway building site, like a bridge or a tunnel |
| *A pay* | Paying out navvies' wages. The navvies often spent it on drink |
| *Barge* | Long, flat-bottomed boat pulled along the canals by horses |
| *Broad gauge* | Rails that had a wide distance between them, more than 4 ft. $8\frac{1}{2}$ in. |
| *Cholera* | A killer disease. It spread where water supplies were polluted |
| *Contractors* | Men who offered to build a tunnel or bridge at a fixed price and then hired the navvies to do the job |
| *Cutting* | Long and deep path through a hillside for the tracks |
| *Director* | One of the group of men who managed the railway companies |
| *Enquiry* | A special investigation, usually by government inspectors, after an accident |
| *Footplate* | Driver's and fireman's platform on an engine |
| *Friction* | Resistance between something moving and something still which slows up the moving object |

| | |
|---|---|
| *Geologist* | An expert on the rocks which make up the earth's crust |
| *Gradient* | Special railway word for a slope |
| *Investor* | Someone who loaned money to the railways by buying shares |
| *Junction* | A station where two or more railway lines meet |
| *One-in-twelve* | Measure for gradients. The slope goes up or down one unit for every twelve units travelled |
| *Maim* | To cripple |
| *Navvy* | A railway builder who laid the track and made the tunnels, cuttings and embankments |
| *Poaching* | Catching fish or game illegally |
| *Retaining wall* | Brick wall built up the steep sides of a cutting to stop rocks falling |
| *Shaft* | The great hole navvies bored into the hillside to start their tunnels |
| *Share* | A way of loaning money to a company. The lenders get shares in return which entitles them to a part of the company's profits. Shareholders are also allowed to vote at meetings and have a say in running the company |
| *Stemmer* | Navvy who had the dangerous job of packing gunpowder into holes drilled in the rock |
| *Survey* | Mapping out the route for a new railway |
| *Terminus* | A large city station at the end of a line |
| *Toll* | Money paid by travellers to use a bridge or a road |
| *Tramway* | An early horse-drawn railway |

# More Books

Coleman, Terry. *The Railway Navvies* (Pelican, 1965). The best book about the navvies—how they lived and worked during the age of railway building. For older readers.

Ferneyhough, Frank. *Railways* (Wayland, 1970). The story of railways from Stephenson's *Rocket* to the trains of the 1970s, with hundreds of pictures. For older readers.

Hastings, Paul. *Railroads, an International History* (Benn, 1972). For those of you who want to learn how the Canadian-Pacific, Trans-Siberian and other great railways in foreign countries were built.

*I Spy on a Train Journey* (Dickens Press, 1973). An ideal book to take with you the next time you travel by train. It will show you what to look out for on the journey.

Morgan, Bryan. *The Railway Lover's Companion* (Eyre & Spottiswoode, 1962). A wide range of stories about the railways, including descriptions of engineers, navvies, bridges, tunnels, accidents and excursions.

*Railways* (MacDonald Junior Reference Library, 1969). A history of the railways—how they were built and how they are run.

# Index

## Picture Credits

The publishers wish to thank the following for their kind permission to reproduce copyright illustrations on the pages mentioned: Science Museum, London, 6, 8, 10, 11, 12, 13, 15, 16, 17, 21, 22, 23, 25, 26, 29, 31, 32, 34, 37, 38, 40, 42, 43, 44–45, 46, 47, 50, 51, 52, 53, 54, 56, 57, 58, 63, 65, 77, 83, 85 (top), 86, 87; Trustees of the British Museum, 9; Mary Evans Picture Library, 14, 18, 24, 30, 33, 34, 41, 60, 66, 67, 68, 70, 81; British Rail, 20, 73, 76; Radio-Times Hulton Picture Library, 28, 48, 55, 59, 61, 64, 78–79; Trustees of the London Museum, 35; Mansell Collection, 62; By courtesy of the Post Office, 74; London Transport Board, 75; W. H. Smith, 88; Birmingham City Art Gallery, 90. Other illustrations appearing in the book are the property of the Wayland Picture Library.